: crafts

# nordic crafts

over 30 projects inspired by Scandinavian style

**Mia Underwood**

**CICO BOOKS**

LONDON NEW YORK

This book is to celebrate the life of my "mormor" Lilly Graversen, and inspiration from my beautiful mother Birgit Underwood.

Published in 2013 by CICO Books
An imprint of Ryland Peters & Small Ltd
20–21 Jockey's Fields          519 Broadway, 5th Floor
London WC1R 4BW              New York, NY 10012

www.rylandpeters.com

10 9 8 7 6 5 4 3 2 1

A CIP catalog record for this book is available from the
Library of Congress and the British Library.

ISBN: 978 1 78249 046 3

Printed in China

Editor: Becky Alexander
Designer: Geoff Borin
Photographer: Jo Henderson
Stylist: Sophie Martell
Illustrator: Michael Hill
Templates: Stephen Dew

For digital editions, visit www.cicobooks.com/apps.php

# contents

Introduction 6

Techniques and stitches 8

# introduction

This collection of projects is inspired by traditional and modern designs from Denmark, Norway, Sweden, and Finland. There are items for the home, for children, for playtime, and for the different celebrations that punctuate the year.

As a child, visiting my mother's parents in Copenhagen, I used to love going to see my "mormor" or grandmother. One thing I particularly liked was the smell of freshly-baked cinnamon buns and coffee, every time you walked through the door. The other was the cupboard in her kitchen, which was just for crafts. My "morfar" or grandfather, constantly told her it was a mess and she worried that a guest looking inside would get a shock, but I thought it was so exciting. I was always curious to find out what project she had next for my cousins and I to make together. She had a cutting mat and templates, articles cut out from magazines, all sorts of bits and pieces. Nobody else I knew had a "crafty cupboard," and I loved it.

The visits to Denmark were also an eye opener when it came to finding inspiration–when we went into a local book store and hobby center, it had an extensive collection of supplies and project ideas, which I had never seen back home. I always tried to record my ideas for new projects in a sketchbook.

The Nordic countries are still very keen on their cozy crafts, creating clothes, accessories, and decorations by hand for the bitter cold weather. They are also known for being really good at creating a cozy atmosphere—it is such a fundamental aspect of Danish culture that they even have a special word for it, "hygge."

In this book I have tried to re-create the pleasure of those days spent making things at my grandmother's kitchen table, and also to celebrate the best of Nordic design, old and new. With Nordic crafts the focus is on natural materials, with simple lines and not too much detail or bright colours. Nature and the outdoors are key influences. Nordic people take a lot of pride in their handmade craftsmanship, which is why it is widely appreciated throughout the world.

I hope these projects spur you on to roll up your sleeves and get crafting. It is good for the soul, rewarding, therapeutic, and a great way to connect and build loving memories with friends and family. To be given something handmade is, I think, the best gift of all.

Put the kettle on, get those creative juices flowing, and get making!

# techniques and stitches

The projects in this book are made using a number of different crafts and techniques. In addition to the step-by-step instructions for each project, here are detailed instructions for the basics of each craft.

# needle-felting

Needle-felting is a simple craft to learn, with very effective results. You just need some wool, a felting needle, and a foam pad to get started.

### felting needle and handle

Felting needles are very sharp and should be kept away from children: needle-felting isn't a suitable craft for young children to try. The needles are made from carbon steel and are about 3 in. (8 cm) long. The L-shaped hook fits into a handle and the barbed sharp end does the felting.

The needles come in a variety of sizes, but I have used 38-gauge triangular needles for the projects in this book. **The needles are very sharp**, so it is important to keep your eye on the needle when you are working to avoid poking your finger. You will no doubt accidentally prick yourself with the sharp

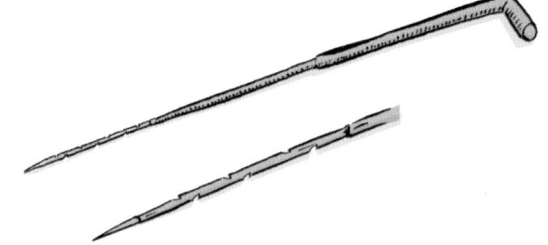

needle a few times to start with, but this will happen less the more you needle-felt and get to know the tool.

The needles are quite fragile; you can insert a needle at any angle into the fibers, but you must bring it up at the same angle or you might break the needle. Using a needle handle helps to prevent the needle from snapping.

### foam pad

A good-quality, firm foam pad will make felting easier. I use large pieces of upholstery foam, although they do degrade after a lot of heavy needling. It is worth investing in a dense foam pad about 1½ in. (4 cm) deep, as this will protect you if you are working on your lap. I prefer to work on a big pad so that my projects are not restricted in size.

## materials

The most commonly used fiber is merino wool, which comes in many different colors. Silkier, softer fibers are harder to felt than coarser, wiry types, which only need a few jabs of the needle to make simple shapes. Never cut fibers before felting, as this will ruin their soft natural edge. Simply pull some wool off the coil with your fingers.

From sheep fleece alone there are different types of wool:

Carded wool is raw wool brushed until the fibers are aligned in the same direction. The fiber is then peeled from the carding brush as a "rolag" that is ready to use.

Wool top is a semi-processed product from raw wool. The wool is scoured (washed), combed, and sorted. The longer fibers resulting from the process are called tops, and are ready for spinning or felting.

A confusion can occur in the use of the terms "tops" and "roving." In the UK, a top is wool that has been carded and combed and is usually about the diameter of thick rope. A roving is the next stage on, where the top has been drawn out to about pencil-thickness. In the USA, tops are often called rovings.

## techniques

**Neeling** The process for turning the soft, fluffy wool into a firm shape is a simple one. A felting needle has special sharp barbs running up from the tip, and this ridged section is called the working zone. Wool is made up of hundreds of tiny fibers; when the needle tip is pushed down into the wool, the barbs catch and move the fibers in the direction you move the needle. This motion tangles and binds the fibers together. The barbs point in only one direction, so as you pull the needle out of the wool the fibers aren't pulled upward. The needle is repeatedly jabbed into the wool, in a motion like the needle in a sewing machine, and by turning the fiber mass on the foam pad while needling, you can create a three-dimensional form. It is important to bring the needle out in the same direction that it went in, to prevent the fragile tip of the needle (which has the notches in it) snapping. As a beginner you will no doubt break a few needles, so you will need to have several on hand for a project, just in case. It is important to hold the needle as comfortably as holding a pen.

Remember to take your time, keep calm, and work at a steady, relaxed pace. Keep your eye on the needle; don't look away or you are more than likely to stab your finger. However, these small pin-pricks tend to heal quickly.

**Starting** Pull off a piece of wool and curl it into a sausage shape. Use the needle to push the curled ends in toward the middle. Hold the fluffy shape with one hand, and with the other hand, jab the needle up and down into the fibre mass.

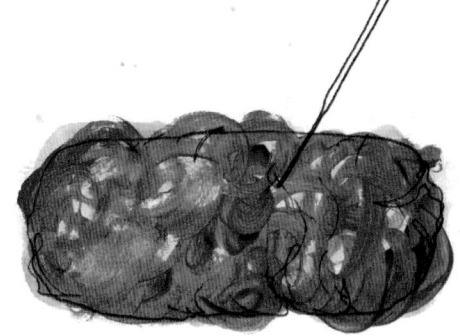

**Shaping** Keep turning the fluffy shape while you work, and squeeze it into shape with one hand while needling it with the other. To make indentations, needle repeatedly over a small surface area.

**Enlarging** Increase an area gradually by wrapping wispy bits of wool over it and needling it all over to attach and smooth out the surface area. Keep adding wool till you get the desired contour.

# mormor's fabric boxes

My mormor (grandmother) must have made hundreds of these boxes, of all different sizes. We used to make them together, along with my mum, aunt, and cousins in my mormor's cozy kitchen. You can use recycled materials, such as old cereal boxes, and offcuts of fabric, and make as many as you like!

**1 Cut out the pieces** Use the templates on page 118 to cut out pieces of cardboard for the base, lid, sides, and lining. Mark on them using pencil which are for the base and which for the lid.

**2 Make the outside of the lid** Place the cardboard for the lid on your chosen fabric for the outside, and draw a circle around, about ½ in. (1 cm) wider than the template. Cut out the fabric, and fold it over the tabs on two opposite sides of the cardboard. Glue down the fabric on the two tabs. Tuck a little piece of batting (wadding) into the center, then glue the fabric on to the remaining four tabs.

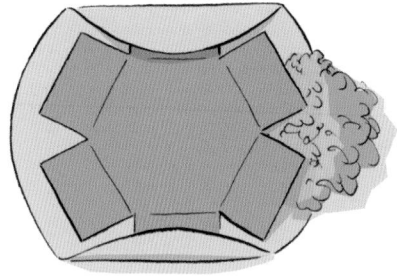

**3 Sew the sides** Tuck the fabric in between two tabs. Hold the fabric between your forefinger and thumb with one hand, and sew the sides together using your other hand. Use matching thread, and tiny stitches, as they will be visible. Continue around with the other tabs. Trim off the excess fabric from the inside.

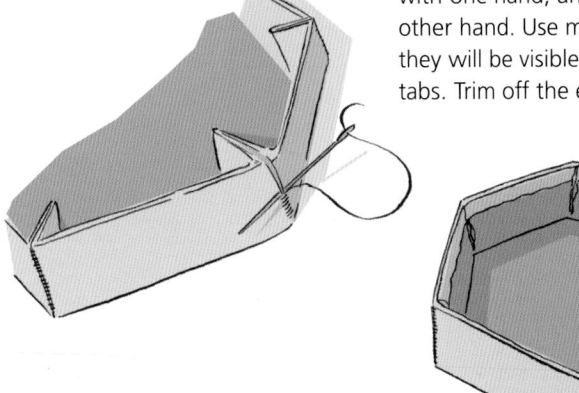

**4 Make the inside of the lid** Place the hexagon-shaped piece of cardboard for the inside of the lid on a piece of the inside fabric, and cut around the fabric as before. Put a little batting (wadding) between the fabric and the cardboard, then fold over the edges and glue into position.

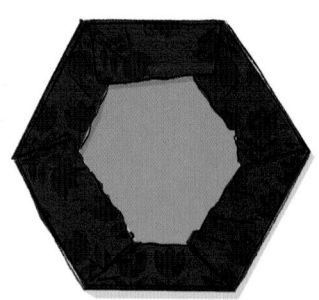

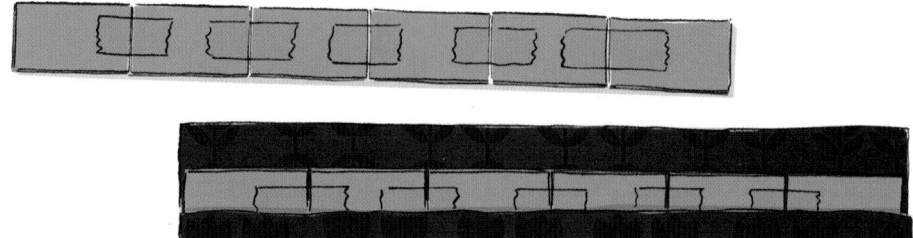

**5 Make the sides** Cut six rectangles, using the template on page 118. Each rectangle should be the size of one side of the lid. Place them in a row alongside each other and stick together using adhesive tape. Cut a strip of fabric just wide enough to fold over the rectangles. Glue the fabric into position.

**6 Fitting the inside of the lid** Sew the bottom of one rectangle to one side of the hexagonal lining piece, then continue around the hexagon until all sides are joined. Place the lining piece inside the box and sew around the top of the sides to join them to the lid, using tiny over stitches.

**7 Make the base** Make the base in the same way as the lid, using the templates on page 118. It will be slightly smaller, to fit inside the lid.

### variation

To decorate the lid, cut out a heart shape from red felt, and pin it to the box lid. Using matching thread, sew around the edge using tiny over stitches.

# fabric bread basket

Fill this lovely bread basket with rolls, croissants, or anything you like! My mormor used to make "tebirkes," delicious breakfast buns with butter and jam. We used to eat them sitting on her porch—happy times!

**1 Cutting the fabric** Cut out a paper pattern using the template on page 119. Pin to the fabric you are using for the outside, draw around the edge using pencil, and cut out. Repeat for the fabric you are using for the inside.

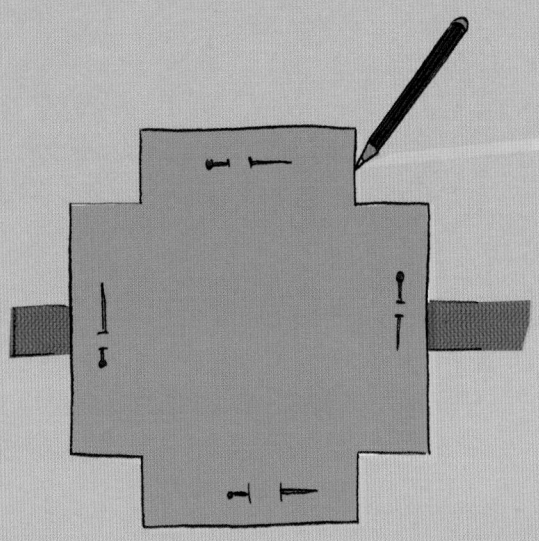

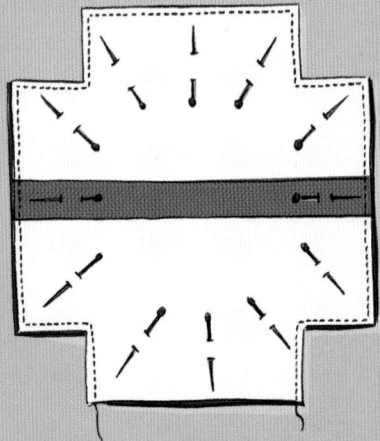

**2 Sewing together** Pin the two pieces of fabric together, with the right sides facing. Use your sewing machine to sew the pieces together, using straight stitch. Leave one side unsewn, so you can turn the pieces the right side out.

## you will need:

Paper for the pattern

Pencil

Scissors

Pins

20 x 20 in. (50 x 50 cm) cotton for the outside, e.g. a linen dish (tea) towel

20 x 20 in. (50 x 50 cm) cotton fabric for the inside

Sewing machine

Approx. 2 yds (2 m) ribbon

16 x 16 in. (40 x 40 cm) batting (wadding)

Small bead or button

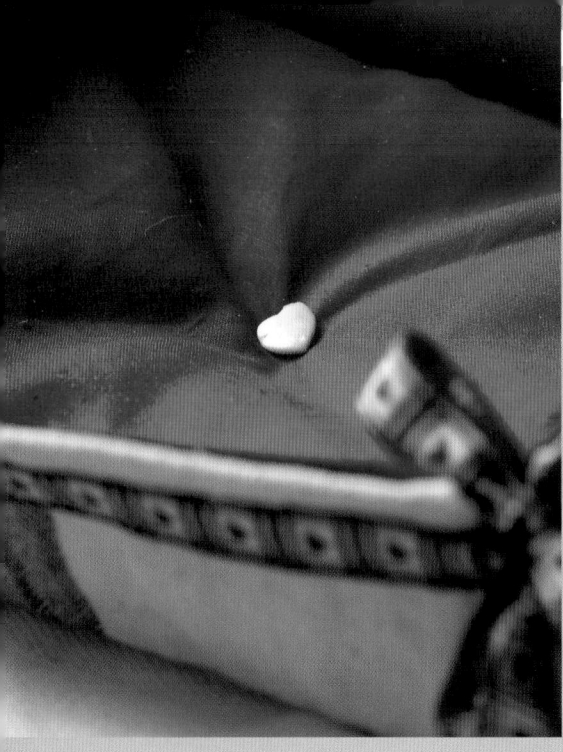

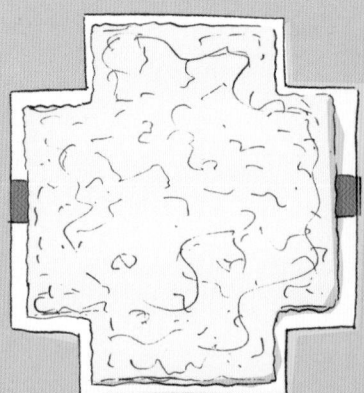

**3 Adding the batting** Cut a piece of batting (wadding) to fit inside the fabric—it will need to be about ½ in. (1 cm) smaller all the way round to fit in. Turn the fabric right side out, and place the batting inside.

**4 Sew up the opening** To close up the unsewn side, fold the fabric inward, about ½ in. (1 cm), and pin. Use the sewing machine to sew the edge using straight stitch.

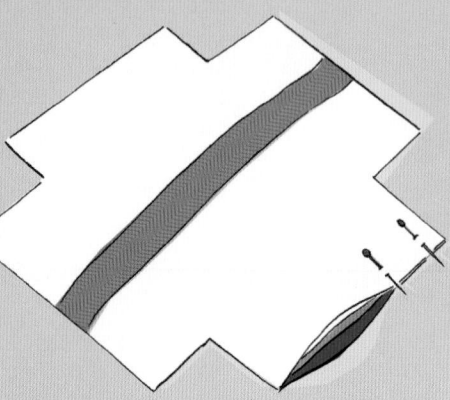

**5 Adding ribbon** Cut the ribbon into 4 equal lengths, each about ½ yd (50 cm). Using the sewing machine set to your choice of decorative stitch, sew each piece of ribbon along one edge of the basket. Leave the ends loose. To bring the basket together, tie the loose ends at each corner into a bow. Sew a small bead or button through the center of the base.

**tip**
You can untie the ribbons and flatten out the basket for easy storage. It is also suitable for washing at a low temperature.

# cat teapot cozy

Cats love staying indoors and keeping warm, so are the perfect personality to keep your teapot cozy throughout the year! I have used a cotton fabric designed by Lotta Jansdotter, who was born in Åland, a small group of islands in the archipelago between Sweden and Finland. Lotta's design aesthetics are deeply rooted in the Scandinavian landscape.

**1 Cut out shapes** Cut out paper patterns using the templates on page 120. Pin the patterns to the fabric and cut out the fabric pieces. You will need 2 x cat shape cut from the decorative front fabric, 2 x inner cat shape cut from the lining fabric, 2 x insulated batting (wadding), and 1 x face shape cut from the lining fabric.

**2 Drawing the face** Use a pencil to draw the features on to the face shape. Cut out two shapes for the eyes from white felt, and pin into position. Sew the white felt into place using a zigzag stitch. Cut out small circles of grey lining fabric for the eye irises, and zigzag stitch these into position as well.

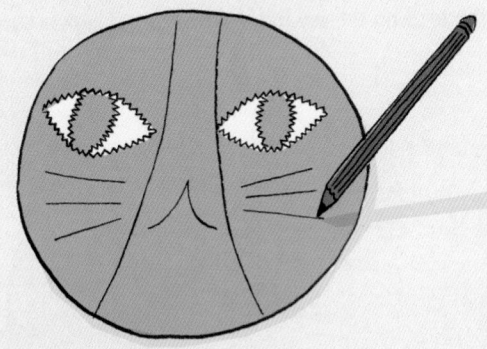

## you will need:

Paper for the pattern

Scissors

Pencil

Pins

Approx ½ yd (50 cm) cotton fabric in your choice of design

Approx ½ yd (50 cm) grey cotton fabric for lining

Approx ½ yd (50 cm) insulated batting (wadding)

Offcut white felt

Sewing machine with white thread

Black mercerized cotton thread

Embroidery needle

Iron

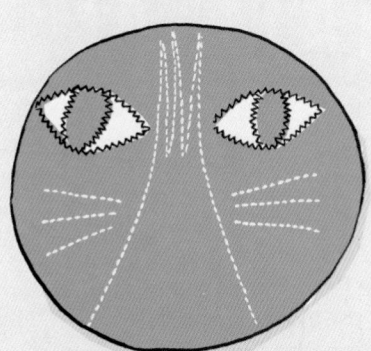

**3 Adding white face features** Use straight stitch to sew on whiskers and the other white decorative lines on the face. When you get to a corner, bring the needle down, lift up the foot, and turn the fabric on the needle to keep the sewing line consistent.

# circular crochet rug

This rug is inspired by Swedish rag rugs that are usually made with fabric strips cut from unwanted clothes or sheets. For this project I used a fantastic yarn called Zpagetti by Hooooked that creates a similar effect; they have a great range of colors and it is really easy and quick to crochet with. You could also use strips of recycled cotton fabric, tied together. This would make a lovely bath mat, or even a luxurious rug for a pet's bed!

### yarn

1x 850 g cone approx 130 yds (120m) Zpagetti in shade Mix Blue, or use strips of recycled cotton t-shirt about 1in. (2 cm) wide

Contrasting yarn for marker

### you will also need

Crochet hook size US 17 (12 mm)

Large-eyed yarn (wool) needle

Scissors

### abbreviations

Ch = chain; sc = single crochet; dc = double crochet; sl st = slip stitch; st = stitch.

### note

US terms are followed by UK terms in brackets, where they differ.

**1 Getting started**

Ch6 and join with a slip stitch (sl st) to make a circle.

**2 Making rounds**

Mark the first stitch of the next round with a removable stitch marker, so you can see where you start and end a round. Reposition the marker at the beginning of each round to mark the new first stitch. If using recycled fabric, knot each strip on as you need to.

1st round - 2sc (UK: 2dc) into each ch. (12 stitches)

2nd round - * 1sc (UK: 1dc), then 2sc (UK: 2dc) into next st; repeat from * to end of round. (18 stitches)

3rd round - * 2sc (UK: 2dc), then 2sc (UK: 2 dc) in next st; repeat from * to end of round. (24 stitches)

4th round - * 3sc (UK: 3dc), 2sc (UK: 2dc) in next st; repeat from * to end of round. (30 stitches)

5th round - * 4sc (UK: 4dc), 2sc (UK: 2dc) in next st; repeat from * to end of round. (36 stitches)

6th round - * 5sc (UK: 5dc), 2sc (UK: 2dc) in next st; repeat from * to end of round. (42 stitches)

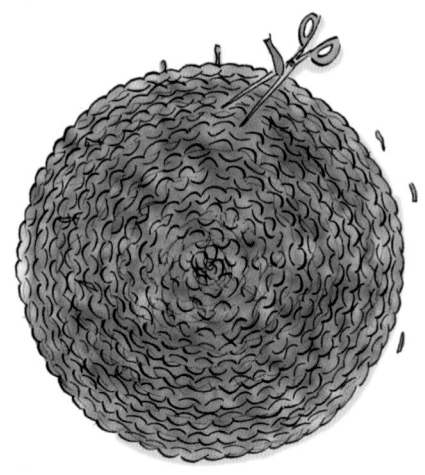

**3 Finishing the rug** Continue with this sequence until you have used up your yarn.

I got to a 15th round, and the rug was 23 in. (59 cm) wide. You can finish there or join on another cone of yarn to make it bigger, and increase in the same sequence. Weave in loose ends with the large-eyed needle, and trim.

**tip**
You can wash this rug safely at a low temperature in a pillowcase cover, or by hand.

# for children

These colorful projects to decorate your child's room, or to be worn, are all inspired by memories of childhood times in Denmark. They include a fairytale mobile featuring characters from the tales of Hans Christian Andersen, and a woodland window hanging that reflects the Nordic love of nature.

# fairytale mobile

Inspired by my wonderful memories growing up in Copenhagen, this mobile features characters from the well-loved Hans Christian Andersen stories **The Little Mermaid** and **The Tinderbox**. You could make just soldiers or just mermaids, of course, or any other favorite fairytale character you wish to make.

## you will need

Felting needle with handle

Needle-felting pad

Approx 3 yd (3 m) red and white string

Large-eyed embroidery needle

8 in. (20 cm) and 4 in. (10 cm) embroidery hoops, wood or painted white with acrylic paint

⅝ in- (1.5 cm-) wide fabric strips, cut from recycled fabric

32 in. (80 cm) ribbon

Sharp scissors

PVA fabric glue

Sewing needle

## for the soldiers

1 oz (25 g) carded washed wool fleece in grey

Small amount of merino wool roving in blue, white, black, red, peach, and light pink

½ oz (10 g) carded washed wool fleece in black

## for the mermaids

1 oz (25 g) carded washed wool fleece in gray

Small amount of merino wool roving in peach, light green, white, blue, light pink, dark pink, and dark green

¾ oz (20 g) dolls' hair in curly blonde

## soldiers

**1 Making the body** Roll a piece of gray fleece wool into a sausage shape about 4 in. (10 cm) long and 1½ in. (4 cm) wide. Jab the shape with the felting needle to make it firm and to tuck in any loose fibers.

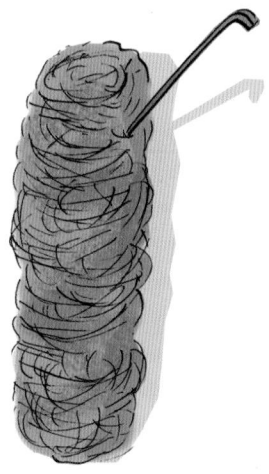

**2 Adding trousers and feet** Wrap a piece of blue wool over one half of the sausage shape. Use the felting needle to jab over the area to make a smooth surface. Needle along the center to create the definition of the legs. Roll a wisp of white wool into a strip using your fingers, and needle into place on either side of the trousers to make a stripe. Use a wisp of black wool around the bottom end of the trousers to make feet.

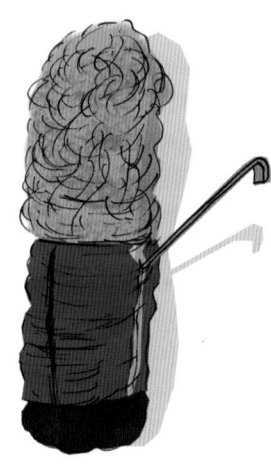

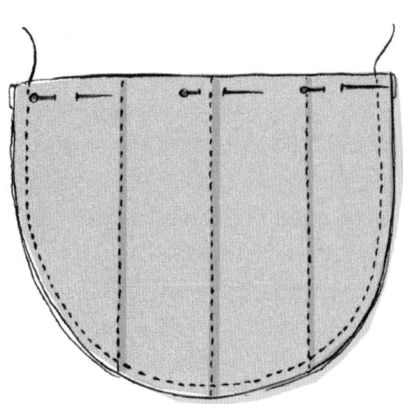

**5 Sewing the pocket** Pin the pocket fabric, lining and batting (wadding) together, wrong sides facing, and sew three lines, evenly spaced as before. Fold down the top edge of the pocket, about ¼ in (5mm), and pin into position. Sew around the edges of the pocket using straight stitch, including across the top to make a neat pocket edge. Trim off any excess fabric, and zigzag stitch around the edge.

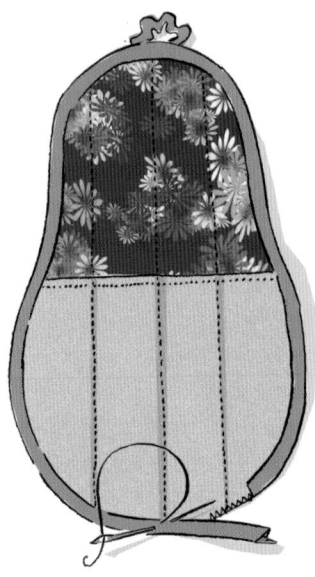

**6 Assembling the bag** Place the pocket on the bag, with the patterned lining fabric on the inside. Pin together. Zigzag stitch around the pocket and bag to hold them together loosely. Place the bias tape around the edge of the bag and pocket, and tack it in place, by hand.

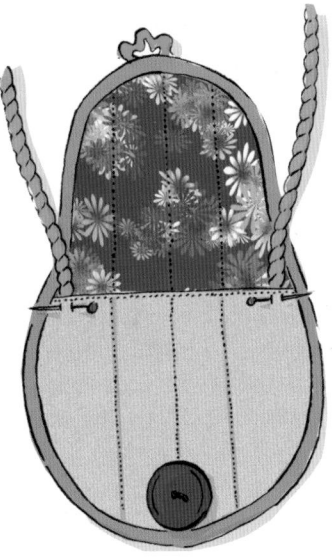

**7 Adding the strap and button** Place the ends of the cord inside the purse and stitch into place, either by hand or using the machine. For extra strength, tuck the ends of the cord into the fold of the bias binding on each side. Carefully machine stitch all around the bias binding using straight stitch, catching the cord ends in place on each side at the same time, making sure the tape lies neatly, especially around curves. Sew the button into place on the front of the pocket. The rikrak "flower stem" is the button loop!

# woodland window hanging

This woodland scene can hang in front of a window, and as the light shines through it will create a stained glass effect. It is also lovely hung simply against a white wall. I made this for my brother's wedding, to represent our Danish roots.

**1 Cutting and pinning the design** Draw inside the hoop on a piece of paper, and sketch out a scene, using the photograph on page 51 for reference. Cut out the stag shape from the green felt using the template on page 119. Cut the strips of linen to various lengths to make Silver Birch tree trunks. You can vary the widths from ¾ in. (1.5cm) to 1¼ in (3cm). Cut the patterned fabric to create a hill shape (you can use the curve of the embroidery hoop as a guide, if you like.) Pin the shapes on to the voile fabric.

**2 Sewing on the shapes** Sew around the hill fabric using the sewing machine set with white cotton using zigzag stitch. Keep the fabric and voile flat with your fingers as you sew. Now sew around the tree trunks. Change to black thread and zigzag around the stag shape.

## you will need

12 in. (30 cm) wood embroidery hoop

Paper for template

Offcut felt fabric in green

Few strips of linen fabric

Offcut of fabric in your choice of pattern (for a hill)

Approx. ½ yd (50 cm) organza voile fabric in beige

Mercerized cotton thread in black

Embroidery needle

Sewing machine with black and white thread

Scissors

Fabric glue

Nylon thread

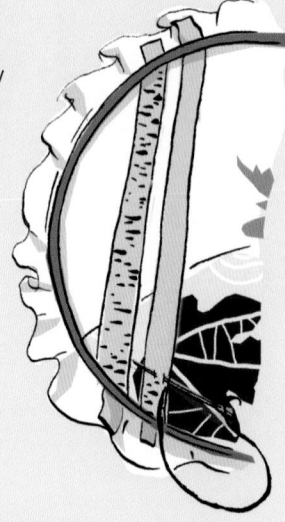

**3 Embroider the bark** Place the voile in the embroidery hoop, and tighten. Use the black mercerized thread and embroidery needle to sew running stitches across the tree trunks, to create a Silver Birch bark effect.

**4 Add branches** Remove the hoop. Using the sewing machine set with white thread, sew branches using zigzag stitch. Go over the branches a few times to make them more solid. You can overlap the stag if you like to make it look as if he is hiding.

**5 Tighten and trim the fabric** When you are happy with your woodland scene, place it back in the hoop. Position the screw at the top of your design. Tighten the screw so the fabric is taut. Trim away any excess fabric, leaving about ½ in. (1 cm) around the edge.

**6 Finishing the hanging** Apply the glue to the inside of the embroidery hoop and fold in the fabric. Stick it down against the hoop and leave to dry. Cut about 12 in. (30 cm) of nylon thread and thread it through the screw at the top. Tie a knot at the end to make a hanging loop.

# daisy stitch baby blanket

This blanket is made with a simple daisy (star) crochet stitch; it takes a while to get into the rhythm but once you get the hang of it, your blanket will grow very quickly. You can use any colors you like, and also vary the width of the stripes to make your blanket unique. It is the perfect size to go on a pram or stroller. The decorative edge is optional (but does look lovely)!

## you will need:

### yarn

2 x 3½ oz (100 g) balls, each approx 220 yd (200 m), Patons Smoothie DK in White 1020 (yarn A)

1 x 3½ oz (100 g) ball, approx, 220 yd (200 m), Patons Smoothie DK in Natural 1091 (yarn B)

1 x 3½ oz (100 g) ball, approx. 220 yd (200 m), Patons Smoothie DK in Slate 1088 (yarn C)

1 x 3½ oz (100 g) ball, approx. 220 yd (200 m), Patons Smoothie DK in Red 1035 (yarn D) for the edging (optional)

## you will also need:

Crochet hook size US 7 (4.5 mm)

Embroidery needle

Scissors

## gauge (tension)

10 daisies (20 stitches) and 12 rows over 4 in. (10 cm) square, using size US 7 (4.5 mm) crochet hook

## abbreviations

sc = single crochet; dc = double crochet; ch = chain; st = stitch

## note

US terms are followed by UK terms in brackets where they differ.

### 1 Making a chain

Using the US 7 (4.5mm) hook and yarn A, make a foundation chain of 93 stitches (an uneven number of stitches is needed for the Daisy stitch pattern).

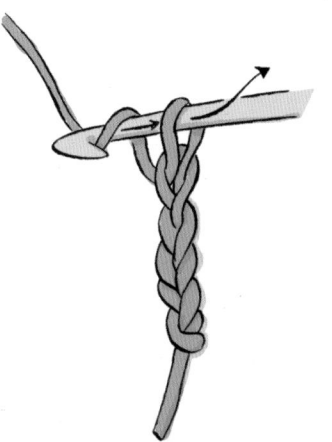

## tip

93 stitches will make 45 daisy stitches. Check the amount of stitches in each row as you work to make sure you keep the number of daisies correct.

# playtime

Playtime is for kids and adults—learn how to have fun away from the television, playing with, and sometimes making, these toys together. There are felted animal masks, traditional "nisse" or gnomes, and a Viking ship to be made. You can even sew a playmat bag, decorated with a snowy woodland scene, to store toys in.

# felt animal masks

Children and adults can wear these masks; they are great for parties and music festivals. I was inspired to make these animal faces from an old wool army blanket and you could use any recycled wool or new felt, or make your own (see page 79). An old jumper could work well! For a perfect fit, cut the template and eye position to suit the wearer.

## you will need

Approx ½ yd (50 cm) cotton fabric for the backing (fabric shown is IKEA cotton "Cecilia"), for each mask

Paper for patterns

Soft pencil

Pins

Small sharp scissors

Fabric glue or glue gun

Sewing needle

Black cotton thread

White cotton thread

12 in. (30 cm) elastic

## for the bear mask

10 x 10 in. (25 x 25 cm) wool blanket or brown felt

8 x 12 in. (20 x 30 cm) sheets of wool felt in black, light brown, dark brown, and light beige

Offcuts of red, pink, and blue felt

## for the owl mask

10 x 10 in. (25 x 25 cm) white wool felt

8 x 12 in. (20 x 30 cm) sheet of wool felt in light beige

6 x 8 in. (15 x 20 cm) sheet of wool felt in dark gray

Offcuts of yellow, pink, black, navy blue, and turquoise felt

## for the fox mask

11 x 11 in. (25 x 25 cm) wool blanket or brown felt

8 x 12 in. (20 x 30 cm) sheet of wool felt in white

6 x 8 in. (15 x 20 cm) sheet of wool felt in black

¼ oz (5 g) white merino wool roving

Felting needle with handle

## sizing guide

Masks fit approx. age 4 years up to adult

**1 Making the templates** Enlarge and copy the templates on pages 122-123 on to paper and cut out to make patterns for the masks. To make sure the wearer can see through the eye holes, hold the paper pattern against the person's face and mark the position of their eyes with a soft felt pen. Remove the mask and cut out the eye holes.

**2 Cutting out the front** Pin the pattern to the wool blanket or felt and draw around the outside using a pencil. Cut out your mask shape; small sharp scissors are ideal, especially for the small tear shapes for the fur and feather details.

**3 Cutting out the back** Cut another shape from the cotton fabric to make a backing—you will need to turn the template the other way round so the backing fits over the top layer.

**4 Adding the features** Cut out the face details from your colored felt sheets and offcuts using the markings on the template (see pages 122–123), and using the pictures on page 58–59 as a guide. Use the fabric glue or glue gun to stick all the face pieces down on to the main base shape.

**5 Sew around the features** Sew around the felt shapes using blanket stitch or an overstitch using black or white cotton thread, to add detail and to secure them in position. Sew around the eyes using blanket stitch in black cotton thread.

**6 Add felted features** For the fox's nose and ears, place a tuft of merino wool roving in position and use a felting needle to press the fibers into position. Keep the wool fairly tufted for a soft, furry texture.

**7 Adding the backing and elastic** Place your cotton fabric on the back of the mask with wrong sides together, and sew around the edge to attach using blanket stitch. When you are level with the eyes, tuck one end of the the elastic in about 1 in. (2.5 cm) and sew between the felt and fabric. Try not to let your stitches show on the front of the mask. Continue with blanket stitch around until you get to the other side, and sew in the other end of the elastic. Finish sewing around the edge.

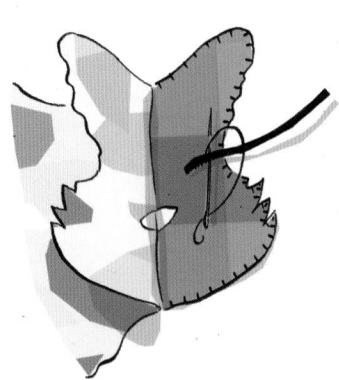

## tip
You can adjust the fit of the elastic by tying a knot in the middle. You can release the knot as the children grow bigger, or when an adult wants to borrow it!

# magical nisse

Nisse are small mythical gnomes who live in the woods and look after your home. These little red-capped figures are so much fun to make and you can add personality with their expressions, hair, and noses. Julenisse bring Christmas presents and like to help with household chores—as long as you leave them a bowl of oatmeal.

**1 Making the body** Pull off a piece of the dark gray or brown wool fleece and roll it into a sausage shape using your hands. Use your felting needle to jab in any loose ends and to shape the body. Make the bottom flat so it can stand up. Add a bit more wool to make a fat tummy if you like.

**2 Adding clothes** Wrap a piece of green wool around the bottom half of the body and use the felting needle to attach it. Jab the needle up and down, and work it over the whole surface to make the wool smooth. Wrap a piece of blue wool around the middle and needle until smooth.

**3 Adding the face** Add a curled wisp of peach wool to make the face and needle until attached and smooth. Add a nose by rolling another wisp of peach wool. Work your needle all around the sides of the nose to attach it. Lightly needle again to make a smooth surface.

Make eye sockets by inserting the felting needle a few times to make an indentation. Roll small pieces of blue wool into two balls with your fingers and use your felting needle to press them into position. Use warm pink wool to add rosy cheeks.

## you will need

¾ oz (20 g) carded washed wool fleece in dark gray or brown, and white, for each nisse

½ oz (10 g) each of merino wool roving in dark green, blue, peach, and warm pink, for each nisse

8 x 12 in. (20 x 30 cm) sheet ready-made felt in red

Felting needle with handle

Sharp embroidery cissors

Cotton thread in red

Sewing needle

**4 Adding hair** Place a piece of white wool fleece underneath the nose and needle it in halfway to create a wispy moustache. Use a generous tuft to make a beard, fastening it under the moustache with a few needle jabs. You can add as little or as much as you like—there are no rules. Add a little wisp of wool on the top of the head to make a fringe that will stick out from under the hat.

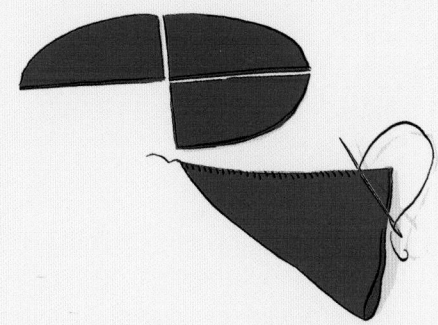

**5 Making the hat** Cut a large circle from the red felt. Fold it into quarters, and cut along the folds to make four pieces. Fold over one piece and sew blanket stitch along the long edge using red thread and a sewing needle. Turn the hat inside out and try it for size—if it is too big, cut around the bottom edge to make it smaller, before finishing off the stitching, or fold it to make a brim.

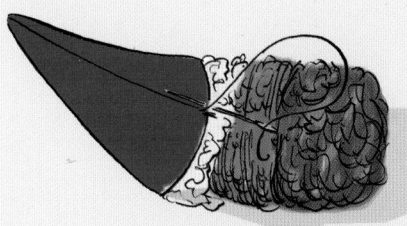

# Nisse lady

If you would like to make a girl nisse, you will need strands of merino wool for the hair: purple, white, or cream work well. To attach wool strands, lay them flat across the head and use your felting needle to attach down the middle, making a parting. Tie into bunches with colored yarn or thread if you like! Add a tiny rolled ball of red or dark pink for lovely lips.

**6 Adding the hat** Place the hat onto your nisse and push the head into it. Stitch the hat in place. You can disguise the stitches if you like by covering with a little more white wool.

# felt circus animals

When I was about eight years old my mormor (grandmother) gave me a kit to make a lion's head from felt pieces. I have based this project on that memory, as I love its simplicity and charm. This is a nice project for older children and adults to make. If you prefer, you can glue on the details, rather than stitch. You can use it as a puppet, for a wall hanging, or as a toy to go with the playmat on page 73.

## note

If making this for children aged under three years old, replace the beads with stitches to make the eyes and badge.

## you will need

Sewing needle

Small sharp scissors

Soft pencil to draw on felt

Fabric glue/pva

Handful of fiberfill stuffing

## lion

6 x 8 in. (15 x 20 cm) sheets of felt in dark yellow and tangerine

Offcuts of felt in white, yellow, navy blue, light blue, pink, red, and cream

2 x black beads

8 x silver tube beads

Fabric glue

Gold metallic thread

Black, white, and dark yellow cotton thread

8 in. (20 cm) embroidery floss (thread) in orange, silver, and pink

## bear

6 x 8 in. (15 x 20 cm) sheet of felt in brown

4 x 6 in. (10 x 15 cm) sheet of felt in turquoise blue

Offcut of red felt

Star-shape bead

Gold metallic thread

Brown, black and red cotton thread

2 x black beads

## tip

When stuffing the circus animals with stuffing, use the end of a pencil to push it into small areas.

## lion

**1 Cut out felt pieces** Using the template on page 120 as a guide, cut the body from the dark yellow felt. You will need two pieces—when you have cut the first piece, turn over the template to cut out the back of the lion. Cut out the head shapes from tangerine felt (you will need two the same size). Cut out the legs from the dark yellow felt. Cut out the face from the white felt, cheeks from the pink, tip of the nose from the navy blue, and the rest of the nose from the light blue. Cut out the paws from the cream felt.

**2 Stitching the face** Using the gold thread, stitch the face features on to the face shape, using the illustration as a guide. Keep the stitches small and tidy. Sew on the black beads for the pupils, and the silver tube beads for the surrounding crosses, with matching cotton. Cut offcuts of felt into small triangles and glue around the edge of the face to add a colorful ruff.

**3 Making a tail** Knot the orange, silver, and pink embroidery floss (threads) together at one end, and braid (plait) together. Tie at the bottom, leaving a few strands. Pierce a tiny hole in the back body piece and insert the braided tail. Stitch into place inside the back piece using matching cotton thread.

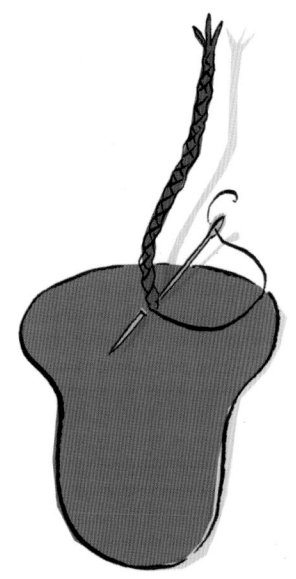

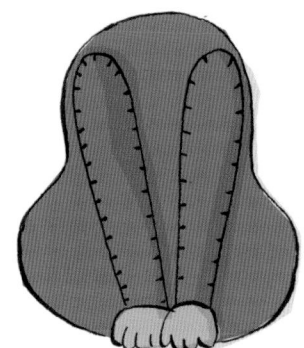

**4 Adding legs and paws** Stitch the lion legs on to the front body piece using blanket stitch, and matching cotton thread. Stitch on the paws and add extra stitches to define the claws.

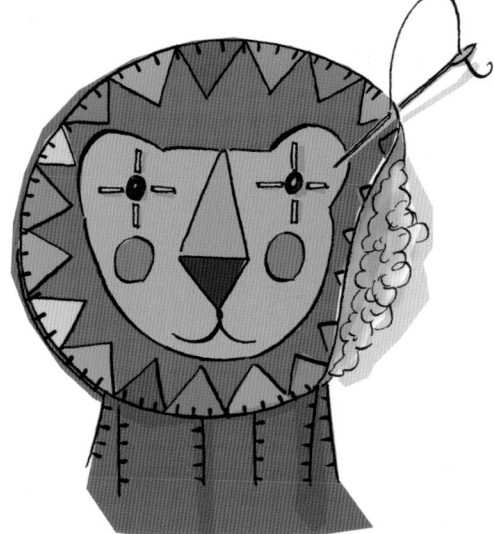

**5 Sewing together** Place the body pieces together and sew around the edge using blanket stitch and matching thread until about halfway round. Insert some fiberfill stuffing. Continue to sew around.

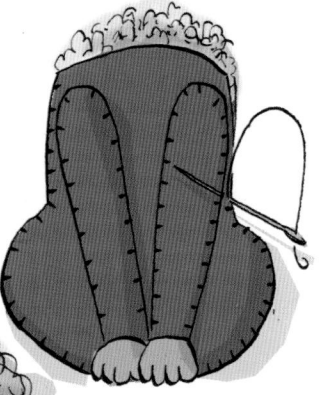

**6 Adding the head** Place the body between the front and back head shapes. Sew the head about halfway around using blanket stitch, with metallic gold thread. Fill with fiberfill stuffing, then continue around. As you sew around you will also help fix the triangles on the front of the face.

# bear

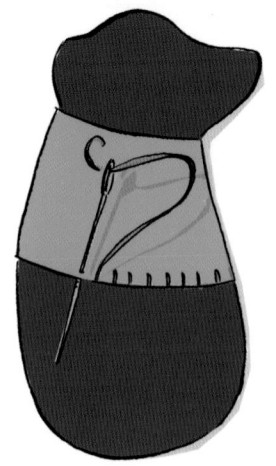

**1 Cut out felt pieces** Using the templates on page 120, cut out two body shapes, four leg shapes and two paw shapes from the brown felt. Cut out two jacket pieces and two sleeve pieces from the turquoise blue felt. Cut out two triangle shapes from the red felt for the hat.

**2 Stitching the body and jacket** Place one jacket piece onto a body piece and sew into place using blanket stitch and metallic gold thread. Repeat with the other side, making sure that the jacket is on the outside of each body part.

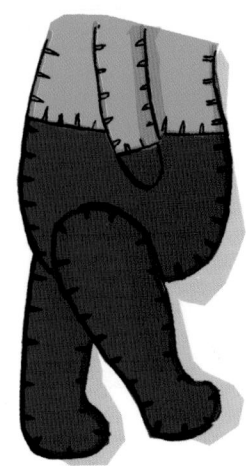

**3 Adding the paws and sleeves** Place one sleeve piece onto one side of the jacket, place one paw just under the end of the sleeve, and stitch both into place using blanket stitch and metallic gold thread. You can insert a little stuffing under the sleeve to plump up the shape. Repeat on the other side. Sew the star bead onto the front of the jacket.

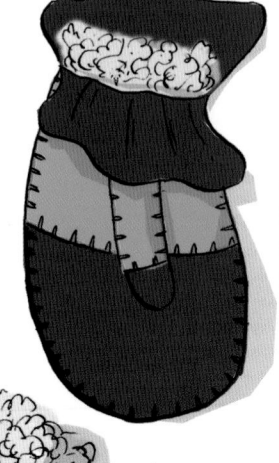

**4 Sew the body together** Sew the body shape together using an overstitch and brown cotton thread until about halfway round, and then fill with fiberfill stuffing. Continue to sew around.

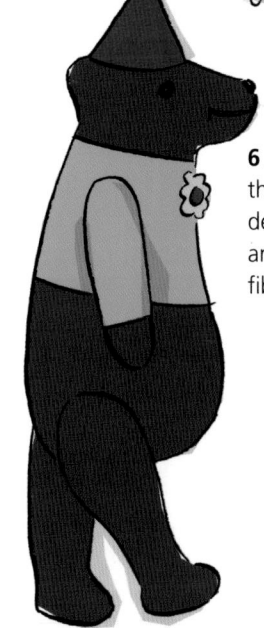

**5 Adding the legs** Sew together two leg pieces, filling with fiberfill stuffing as you sew. Repeat for the other leg. Sew the legs onto either side of the body in a standing position.

**6 Adding a face and hat** Sew on the black beads for eyes and then sew a few stitches on both sides for the mouth and nose detail using black thread. Sew the red triangles onto the head and around the edges using red thread, filling with a small piece of fiberfill stuffing as you sew.

## tip
To make your circus animals into hanging ornaments to decorate your child's room, sew a loop of ribbon or thread to the inside of the bear's hat or the top of the lion's head.

# viking ship

Show your children how to recycle cardboard packaging and scraps of fabric into this Viking long ship; I think every young child would love a hand-made ship to play with, especially if they have helped to make it. This is a simple design and you can make it to whatever scale you want. It won't float in water, but will be fantastic for imaginary play.

**note** Due to small parts, only suitable for age 4+

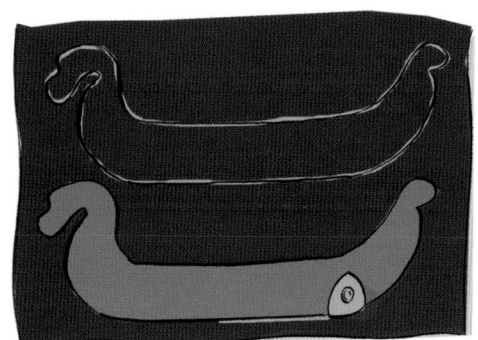

**1 Cutting out the cardboard** Using the templates on pages 124–125, cut out two pieces of the cardboard to make the sides of the boat, one piece of cardboard to make the base of the boat, and one piece to make the deck. Using the pieces of cardboard as a template, draw around the sides and base on the wool blanket or brown felt using a soft pencil or chalk. Add an extra ¾ in. (2cm) all round. Cut out.

**2 Joining the cardboard pieces** Tape the bow (head) and stern (tail) of the cardboard sides together using clear adhesive tape, then tape the cardboard base of the boat to the sides.

## you will need

24 x 40 in. (60 x 100 cm) cardboard

Scissors

Approx 2 yd (2 m) recycled wool blanket or brown felt

Chalk or soft pencil

Adhesive clear tape

Glue (UHU, PVA)

Sewing and embroidery needles

White string

14 x large buttons for shields

Black, white, and metallic gold floss (thread)

Felt offcuts in green, light green, black, yellow, orange, and red

Cotton reel or cork

Plant stick

12 x 13 in. (30 x 33 cm) red and white striped fabric

Scraps of fabric

2 x wood skewers

Red adhesive tape or felt

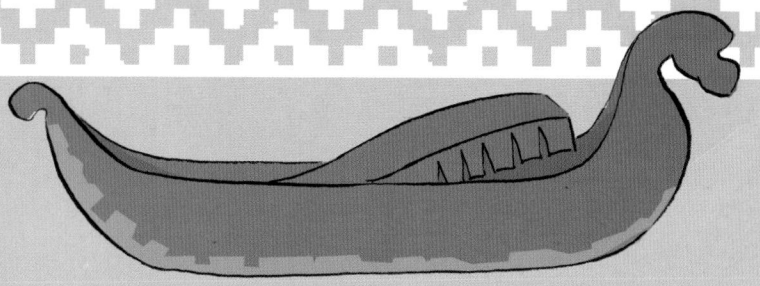

**3 Insert decking** Snip around the edges of the cardboard deck piece, fold in the sides, and slide it inside the boat to make a deck.

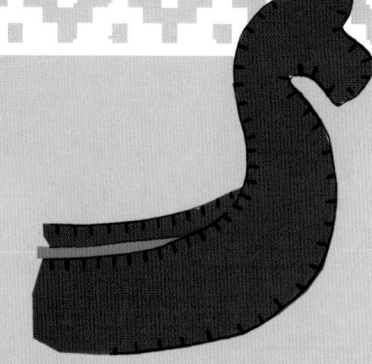

**4 Attaching the fabric** Glue the fabric on to the sides of the boat, folding over at the top of each side. Blanket stitch around using black thread to attach to the cardboard. Repeat on the other side. Sew the base fabric on to the fabric sides. When you come to curved sections, snip a few slits into the edge of the fabric to make folding over the fabric easier and neater.

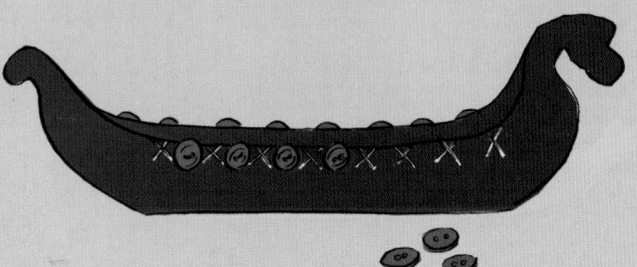

**5 Add details** Sew eight cross-stitches on each side using white string. Sew on buttons between the stitches to make shields.

**6 Add ears, face, and tail** Cut out two "tear" shape pieces of blanket or brown felt, and stitch into place to form the ears. Use colored offcuts of felt to add eyes, nostrils, and tongue as shown. You can also add green or multi-colored spikes down the spine, and add a tail too.

**7 Adding the mast** Cut out another piece of blanket or felt to fit over the deck of the boat. Before you glue into place, cut out a hole about the size of your cotton reel or cork in the center. Glue the fabric on the deck, tucking it in around the edges. Glue the cotton reel or cork on top of the hole so it attaches to the cardboard. Insert the plant stick for the mast, adding a dab of glue to secure it, if needed.

**8 Making the sail** Cut out scraps of fabric to make a design to go on the sail. Glue the pieces in place first if you like, then stitch around the edge using metallic gold thread. For the Viking hat design shown here, attach the hat and horn shapes first. Cut out a "T" shape, and glue into place, then finish with small circles to look like rivets along the base of the hat. An initial or number would look good too.

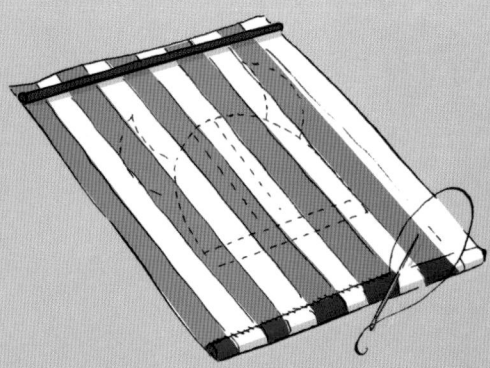

**9 Adding the sail** Turn the sail fabric so it is facing right side down. Place one wood skewer near the bottom, and fold about ½ in. (1 cm) fabric over it. Sew along with white thread. Repeat for the top.

**10 Attach the sail** Attach the sail to the mast by sewing over it using white thread. Add a small piece of red adhesive tape or felt to the top of the mast for the Viking flag

**tip**
You can paint your own red-and-white striped fabric if you like.

# playmat toy bag

Perfect for young children, this toy bag with its own playmat on the front can travel with you anywhere, whether going to a picnic, a friend's house, or on a train or plane. You can store toys inside, such as wood animals or vehicles, or you could make the felt mermaid and soldier (see page 43), circus bear and lion (see page 64), or pinecone people (see page 108).

## you will need

Paper for the template

Pencil

## for the bag

Approx. ¾ yd (75 cm) pale blue cotton fabric for the front of the bag

Approx. ¾ yd (75 cm) elephant-type print patterned fabric for the back of the bag

Approx. 1½ yd (150 cm) cotton fabric for the lining

## for the woodland scene

18 x 7 in. (45 x 18 cm) cotton fabric in star pattern for the sky

Approx. ¼ yd (25 cm) blue fabric (for pond)

18 x 7 in. (45 x 18 cm) green patterned fabric (for mountains)

Offcuts of cotton fabric, e.g. blue, red polka dot, and patterned green leaves

Offcuts of felt such as green, black, light green, white, dark brown, light brown, and yellow

Small piece of batting (wadding)

## other

½ yd (50 cm) rikrak in light blue and cyan

Fabric stars, various sizes

16 in. (40 cm) black velcro

1 small decorative button

1 large round button

4 in. (10 cm) of ½ in.- (1 cm-) wide black elastic

Foil first aid blanket

Scissors

Ruler

Fabric glue

Matching thread

**1 Cut out the shapes** Using the templates on page 123, cut out the shapes to go on the playmat side of the bag. Cut a rectangle 18 x 22 in. (45 x 55 cm) from the pale blue fabric for the base color of your woodland scene on the front of the bag. Cut another rectangle the same size from your patterned fabric for the back of the bag. Cut a rectangle of 18 x 43 in. (45 x 108 cm) from the lining fabric.

**2 Add the main shapes** Pin the star fabric across the top of the pale blue fabric. Using the sewing machine set with white thread, zigzag stitch along the bottom. Cut a little batting (wadding) slightly smaller than the mountain shapes. Pin the mountains into position, with the batting underneath, and zigzag stitch around.

**3 Fo**

Cut
yarn
yarn

**5 Fe**

Plac
was
slipp
a pe

**Add**

Use
tie a
the
edg

chapter 4

# cozy time

Nordic countries are famous for their long, dark winters, so the people there know a thing or two about keeping warm. These lovely projects will keep you cozy during the cold months. There are hats, a snood, and scarves to wrap up in. You can knit yourself a pair of toasty-warm socks, or even make your own felted slippers.

## yarn:

1 (1) 1 (1) 2 (2) 2 (2) x 1¾ oz (50 g) balls, each approx. 230yds (210m), of Regia 4 ply (75% virgin wool 25% Polyamide)

Embroidery floss (thread) in pale gray

## you will also need

A set of 5 double-pointed needles in size US 1 or 2 (2.5 mm)

A set of 5 double pointed needles in size US 2 or 3 (3 mm)

Embroidery needle and thread

Scissors

## gauge (tension):

28 stitches and 36 rows to 4 in. (10 cm) square in stockinette (stocking) stitch using size US 2 or 3 (3 mm) needles.

## abbreviations:

k = knit; p = purl; sl = slip; st = stitch; psso = pass slipped stitch over; tog = together

## sizes:

2 (4) 6 (8) 10 (12) years, woman (man)

# knitted socks

My mormor (grandmother) used to knit socks for the whole family, and this is her tried-and-tested pattern. My Dad used to get excited getting these socks for Christmas! They fit your feet perfectly and feel so soft and comfy...what a cozy treat!

### 1 Casting on

Cast on: 40 (44) 48 (52) 56 (60) 64 (68) stitches using size US 1 or 2 (2.5 mm) stocking needles and distribute the stitches evenly between four needles—10 (11) 12 (13) 14 (15) 16 (17) sts on each needle. Work 2 in. (5 cm) in the round in rib stitch as follows: Every round: *k1, p1 * repeat to end of fourth needle.

Change to size US 2 or 3 (3 mm) needles and work in the round in stockinette (stocking) stitch (k all stitches, when knitting in the round) until knitting measures 2¾ (3) 3½ (4) 4¾ (5½) 6¼ (7) in. / 7 (8) 9 (10) 12 (14) 16 (18) cm, finishing at the end of a round.

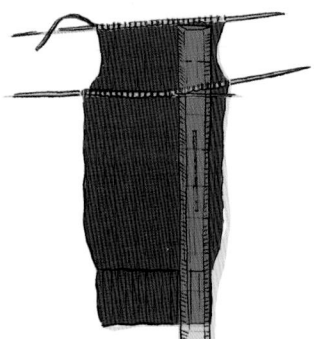

### 2 Starting the heel

Knit across the 10 (11) 12 (13) 14 (15) 16 (17) sts on first needle. Now, knit across 2nd then 3rd needles— 20 (22) 24 (26) 28 (30) 32 (34) stitches—so the stitches on 2nd and 3rd needle end up on one needle. Work backward and forward on these stitches in normal stockinette (stocking) stitch for the heel, until it measures 1¼ (1⁵⁄₁₆) 1½ (1¾) 2 (2¹⁄₁₆) 2³⁄₁₆ (2½) in. / 3 (3.5) 4 (4.5) 5 (5.5) 6 (6.5) cm ending with a purl row.

### 3 Shaping the heel

Continue on these 20 (22) 24 (26) 28 (30) 32 (34) sts and work backward and forward in stockinette (stocking) stitch:

Row 1: K14 (15) 16 (17) 19 (20) 21 (22) stitches, sl1, k1, psso, turn and leave the remaining stitches on the needle.

Row 2: Sl1, p8 (8) 8 (8) 10 (10) 10 (10) stitches, p2tog, turn and leave the remaining sts on the needle.

Row 3: Sl1, k8 (8) 8 (8) 10 (10) 10 (10) stitches, sl1, k1, psso, turn and leave the remaining sts on the needle.

Repeat rows 2 and 3 until 10 (10) 10 (10) 12 (12) 12 (12) sts remain, finishing with a purl row.

Divide these stitches over 2 needles.

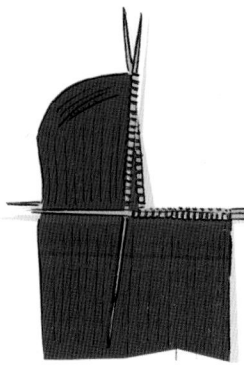

### 4 Starting the foot

Round 1: K5 (5) 5 (5) 6 (6) 6 (6) stitches and leave on the needle. With the next needle knit across the remaining 5 (5) 5(5) 6 (6) 6 (6) stitches, then on same needle pick up and knit 10 (11) 12 (13) 15 (17) 18 (20) stitches along straight row-ends of the heel. With next needle k across 10 (11) 12 (13) 14 (15) 16 (17) sts and with another needle k across next 10 (11) 12 (13) 14 (15) 16 (17) sts.

With next needle pick up and knit 10 (11) 12 (13) 15 (17) 18 (20) sts along straight row-ends of the heel and knit across the last 5 (5) 5 (5) 6 (6) 6 (6) sts. Rounds now end at center of heel.

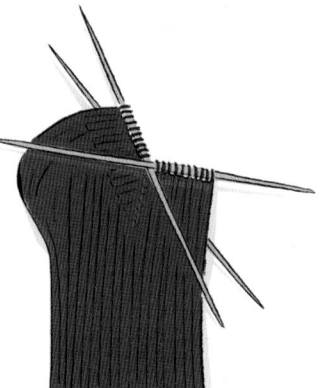

### 5 Knitting the foot

Round 2: 1st needle: k13 (14) 15 (16) 19 (21) 22 (24) stitches, k2tog. Knit across the stitches on 2nd needle. Knit across the stitches on 3rd needle. 4th needle: sl1, k1, psso, k13 (14) 15 (16) 19 (21) 22 (24) stitches.

Round 3. Knit.

Round 4: 1st needle: k12 (13) 14 (15) 18 (20) 21 (23), k2tog. Knit across the stitches on 2nd needle. Knit across the stitches on 3rd needle. 4th needle: sl1, k1, psso, k12 (13) 14 (15) 18 (20) 21 (23) stitches.

Round 5: Knit.

Carry on decreasing on next and every second row to make one less stitch on 1st and 4th needles until 10 (11) 12 (13) 14 (15) 16 (17) stitches are left on each of the needles and 40 (44) 48 (52) 56 (60) 64 (68) stitches are left in total on the 4 needles.

Carry on knitting straight without any decreasing until the work measures 4¼ (5¼) 6 (6½) 7¼ (8) 8¾ (9½) in. / 11 (13) 15 (16) 18 (20) 22 (24) cm, measuring from the back of the heel.

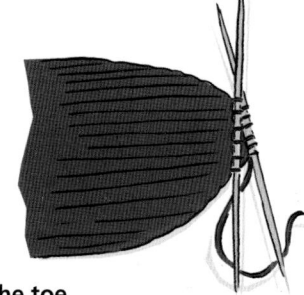

### 6 Shaping the toe

Round 1: *Next needle, k7 (8) 9 (10) 11 (12) 13 (14), k2tog, k1; next needle k1, sl1, psso, k7 (8) 9 (10) 11 (12) 13 (14)*, repeat from * to * once.

Round 2: Knit.

Round 3: *Next needle, k6 (7) 8 (9) 10 (11) 12 (13), k2tog, k1; next needle k1, sl1, psso, k6 (7) 8 (9) 10 (11) 12 (13)*, repeat from * to *once.

Round 4: Knit.

Carry on decreasing like this on next and every second row until 12 (12) 12 (12) 16 (16) 20 (20) sts are left in total on all the needles. Flatten the toe, with shaping at outer edges. Sew the 2 x 6 (6) 6 (6) 8 (8) 10 (10) stitches together with mattress (Kitchener) stitch (see page 14).

Knit the second sock in the same way.

**tip**
Keep the back of your work tidy and knot-free to keep it smooth, so the sock is comfortable to wear.

### 7 Embroidery detail

Using pale gray embroidery floss (thread), embroider the socks with lazy daisy stitches (see page 19.) Start by the ankle area of each sock. Each petal is three knit stitches long, and each flower is three knit stitches apart. On the back of the sock use feather stitch (see page 19) to create a vine the same length as the flower strand.

# tree of life fingerless gloves

Transform plain accessories into exquisite unusual items with simple embroidery stitches. Embroidery is so relaxing and rewarding, and you can create an interesting eye-catching design such as this "tree of life" with just a few simple stitches.

## you will need:

1 pair of plain fingerless gloves

Embroidery floss (threads) in silver or white, and red

Embroidery needle

Sharp scissors

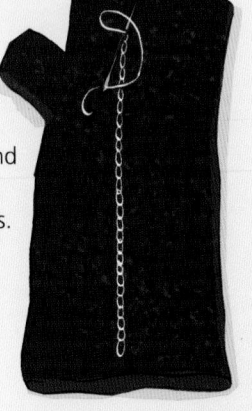

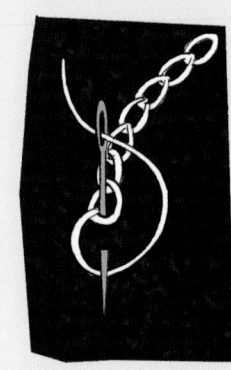

**1 Chain stitch the trunk** Thread your needle with silver or white embroidery floss (thread) and tie a knot in the end. Place one hand inside the glove to prevent you sewing through both sides. Sew a line of chain stitch (see page 19) up the center of the glove, aiming for a total of about 27 stitches.

## tip

Keep thread the length of your arm when sewing—you will find it easier to pull through the fabric, and less likely to tangle.

**2 Add thickness to the trunk** Continue another two lines of chain stitches either side to widen the trunk. I made the second and third chains a little shorter, which looks effective.

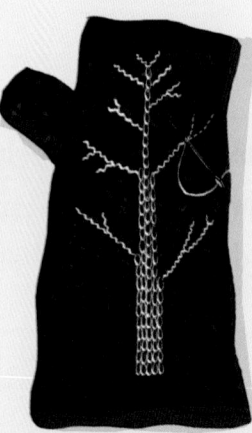

**3 Adding branches** Add eight or nine branches with whipped (threaded) running stitch(see page 18). Continue until you have joined up all the running stitches.

**4 Adding blossom** Thread your needle with red embroidery floss (thread). Sew two stitches in a "v" shape at the end or sides of the branches to add blossom. Add as many or as few as you like. Repeat with the other glove—make them symmetrical if you like!

**5 Coloring the head** Place a generous piece of black wool over the bridge of the beak. Use the felting needle (see felting technique page 9) to press it into place and smooth it out. Shape the end tips of the wool to a point. Make sure both sides of the face look the same.

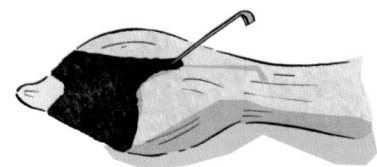

**6 Adding a beak** Curl a large piece of burnt orange wool into a roll. Place it on the foam pad and needle to make a flat shape (2 in.) 5 cm wide and about 3 in. (7.5 cm) long. Rub the shape between your palms to help it to felt and become smooth. Make another the same, but this time roll it into a flat egg shape, curved on both ends. Needle a strip of black wool around both beak shapes for definition.

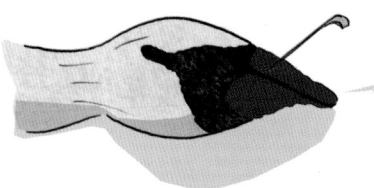

**7 Attaching the beak** Lay the flat piece over the top of the beak and the egg shaped one at the bottom with the narrow end at the tip of the beak. Use the felting needle to join the beak to the head around the edge. Add a few pieces of black wool to build up the black shape on the top part of the beak. You can make this as bulbous as you like.

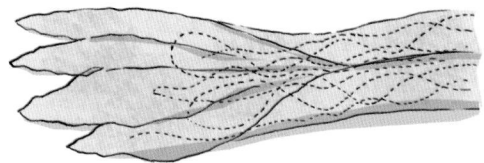

**8 Forming the wing** Open out the wing at the other end of the scarf and sew over the opening to keep the center seam in place. To keep the head stuffing and the rest of the seam in place, and to add a quilted effect, sew up and down the scarf lengthways in a curvy pattern. Add definition and shape to the wing by making some ripples and folds in the felt and sewing them in place.

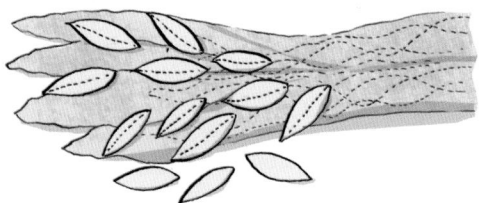

**9 Adding feathers** Cut out teardrop shapes from the extra piece of nunofelt or the white felt. Your feathers can be as long or short, and as many as you like. Place them on the outside of the wing and use the sewing machine to attach them, sewing down the middle of each tear shape.

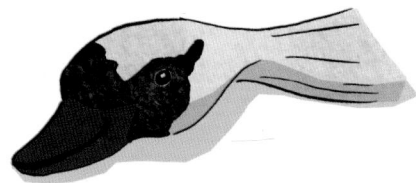

**10 Adding eyes** To finish off, on each side of the head sew on a few iridescent black beads with black thread for the eyes.

# pointed wooly hat

This is a really cute shaped hat, that comes with earflaps! It is a lovely pattern based on a design by my Danish mormor (grandmother,) who used to knit these for all her grandchildren and great-grandchildren. The hat comes together quite quickly and feels really rewarding to knit.

## yarn

2 x 1¾ oz (50 g) balls, each approx 55 yd (50 m), of pure wool light worsted (DK) in your chosen shade

Contrasting yarn for crocheting around the edge and adding Nordic detail

## you will also need

Set of 5 double-pointed needles in size US 11 (8 mm)

Crochet hook size US 6 (4 mm)

Embroidery needle

Scissors

## sizes

Toddler 1-3 years, (child 4 years +), adult

## gauge (tension)

12 stitches and 20 rows to 4 in. (10 cm) square, over stockinette (stocking) stitch using size US 11 (8 mm) double-pointed needles.

## abbreviations:

K = knit; p = purl; kfb = knit into the front and then into the back of the stitch to increase; k2tog = knit two together

---

### 1 Knitting the earflaps

Using two of the size US 11 (8 mm) needles cast on 3 stitches for the earflap.

Row 1: k to end.

Row 2: p to end.

Row 3: Increase 1 stitch (kfb) in the 1st and 2nd stitches, k1. (5 stitches)

Row 4: p to end.

Row 5: k1, increase 1 stitch in next stitch (kfb), k1, increase 1 stitch in next stitch (kfb), k1. (7 stitches)

Row 6: p to end.

Row 7: k1, increase 1 stitch in next stitch (kfb), k to the 2 last stitches, increase 1 stitch in next stitch (kfb), k1.

Row 8: p to end.

Repeat rows 7 and 8 until you have 15 (17) 19 stitches.

Knit 2 rows in stockinette (stocking) stitch without increasing.

Leave the stitches on the needle and set aside. Now repeat from Row 1 for the second earflap.

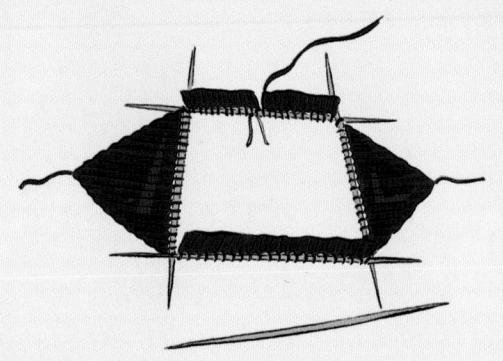

## 2 The hat

Row 1: Start at the back of the hat, by casting on 2 (3) 4 stitches on first size US 11 (8mm) double pointed needle. With second needle, knit across the 15 (17) 19 stitches of one of the earflaps. On third needle, cast on 14 (16) 18 stitches for the front of the hat. On fourth needle, knit across the 2nd earflap, then cast on 2 (3) 4 stitches). (total 48 (56) 64 stitches)

Mark the beginning of the round.

Knit in rounds, using the free fifth needle, until work measures 4 (4½) 5¼ in./10 (11) 13cm, connecting the rounds by knitting into the first stitch of the beginning of the next round.

## 3 Creating the pointed crown

Round 1: *k4, k2tog* (*k5, k2tog*) *k6, k2tog* repeat from *to* to end of round (40 (48) 56 stitches).

Knit 3 rounds without any decreasing.

Round 5: *k3, k2tog* (*k4, k2tog*) *k5, k2tog* repeat from *to* to end of round (32 (40) 48 stitches).

Knit 3 rounds without decreasing.

Round 9: *k2, k2tog* (*k3, k2tog*) *k4, k2 tog* repeat from *to* to end of round (24 (32) 40 stitches).

Knit 3 rounds without decreasing.

Round 13: * k1, k2tog* (*k2, k2 tog*) *k3, k2tog* repeat from *to* to end of round (16 (24) 32 stitches).

Knit 3 rounds without decreasing.

Round 17: *k2, k2tog* (* k1, k2tog*) *k2, k2tog* repeat from *to* to end of round (12 (16) 24 stitches).

Knit 3 rounds without decreasing.

Round 21: * k1, k2tog* (*k2, k2tog*) * k1, k2tog* repeat from *to* to end of round (8 (12) 16 stitches).

For toddler, knit 4 rounds without decreasing and cut the yarn long enough to finish off the crown (about 8 in./20 cm).

For child and adult, knit 3 rounds without decreasing

Round 25: Child and (adult) sizes, only *k1, k2tog* (*k2, k2tog*) repeat from *to* to end of round. (8 (12) stitches)

For child, knit 4 rounds without decreasing and cut yarn long enough to finish off the crown (about 8 in./20 cm).

For adult, knit 3 rounds without decreasing.

Round 29: Adult size only: * k1, k2tog* repeat from *to* to end of round. (8 stitches)

Knit 4 rounds without decreasing and cut the yarn long enough to finish off the crown (about 8 in./20 cm).

Thread the length of yarn through the 8 remaining stitches, using your embroidery needle. Pull tight and fasten the end off on the inside of the hat to make a neat finish. Sew in any loose bits of yarn to finish.

## 4 Finishing touches

Add a decorative edge with a contrast color yarn. You could use a simple blanket stitch, or add a crochet edge. Add heart-shaped stitches too, if you like.

For a crochet edging: starting at the back of the hat, insert your crochet hook into an edge stitch, yarn over hook and pull through to make a loop on the hook. Leave about 6 in. (15 cm) of yarn spare to sew in at the end. Do a slip stitch to join the thread on to the hat to start the crocheted edge.

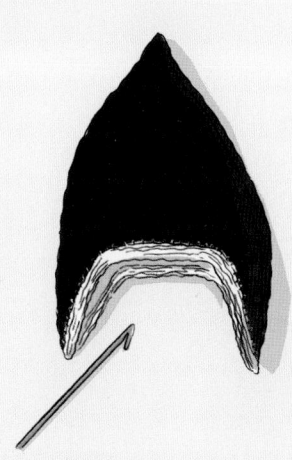

Work around the edge with single crochet (UK double crochet.) When you get to the point on the ear-flaps, chain (ch) 1, and when you finish a round, chain (ch)1. Do a few rounds to make a nice thick edge. Cut the yarn with about 6 in. (15 cm) spare and pull the yarn through the loop on the crochet hook. Sew the loose ends in on the inside of the hat to finish.

For the nordic heart stitch pattern: cut the contrasting yarn about 22 in. (50 cm) long and thread your embroidery needle. Sew two stitches to create a small "V" shape which will look like a heart, following the pattern of the stockinette (stocking) stitch, over every other stitch. Keep the line straight so the "V"s meet to make a perfect ring of hearts. Sew a second ring of hearts two rows above, over the stitches in between the previous round of "V"s. You can use different colored yarns and different size "V"s, to customize your hat.

To finish, use your embroidery needle and work any loose ends of yarn in on the inside of the hat.

# celebrations

Here are some fun ways to decorate your house throughout the year—not just for Christmas—in the Nordic way. Handmade decorations have more character and warmth than shop-bought ones—stitched with love, they are something to cherish and be proud of.

# easter rabbit egg cozy

Perfect for a beginner's sewing project, as felt is so easy to sew; you could make these with children. These cute rabbits will be great for Easter but can also be used all year round to brighten up your breakfast table. Make them whatever color you like; why not make a whole rainbow of bunnies, or add some extra detail for fun, such as daddy's moustache or your family's initials, or add hearts instead of flowers.

## you will need

Paper for template

Pencil

Pins

18 x 22 in. (45 x 55 cm) felt in each of pink and white

Felting needle with handle

Foam pad (you can use upholstery foam)

Small pieces of of black, white, and pink merino roving wool for the eyes, nose, and tail

Embroidery floss (thread) in pink and aqua

Felt offcuts for the flowers

Embroidery floss (thread) in dark green and pale green

Embroidery needle

Scissors

## tip

Suitable for ages 8 years+.
This project is suitable for younger children if you sew or glue the features instead of needle-felting.

**1 Cut out shapes** Cut out a paper pattern using the template on page 119. Pin to the felt, and cut out two rabbit shapes.

**2 Adding an eye** Place one of your rabbit shapes on the foam pad. Roll a small wisp of black merino wool into a ball and place it where you want the eye. Use the felting needle to attach it to the felt, by bringing the needle up and down like a sewing machine. Work the outline first, then jab to press in any loose fibers. Use a wisp of white wool to go around the eye, and to add a dot in the center. Repeat on the other rabbit shape, so the two sides match.

**3 Stitch around the edge** Hold your rabbit pieces together with the right sides facing out. Thread your needle with pink or aqua embroidery floss (thread) and use blanket stitch (see page 19) to join the pieces together. Leave the bottom open. When you get to the ears, sew blanket stitch around the outside of each ear, but don't sew them together. Add a stitch or two between the ears to hold the cozy together at the top.

**4 Adding grass** Use light green embroidery floss (thread) to add grass around the bottom. For each cluster of grass, do three blanket stitches into the same spot. Move along ½ in. (1 cm) to start the next cluster. When you have gone all the way round, fasten off the thread on the inside of the rabbit.

**5 Adding stems** Use dark green embroidery floss (thread) to add flower stems. Start between two clusters of grass, and chain stitch (see page 19) upward about 9 stitches. Add another stem or two, as you like; you could vary the length.

**6 Adding petals** Cut out circles about 1 in. (2.5 cm) in diameter from felt offcuts. Attach the circles above the stems by bringing your needle up through the center, and taking it out to the sides. Use a complementary or contrasting embroidery floss (thread). If you pull the floss (thread) in as you sew it will pucker the felt circle to create a petal shape.

**7 Adding a nose** Roll a small ball of pink merino wool and use the felting needle to attach it either side of the rabbit's head.

**8 Adding a tail**
Roll a small ball of white merino wool and needle it together on the foam pad to make it firm. Needle it into position on the rabbit's bottom. You can add a little more wool to add fluff, and to cover and reinforce the join.

# easter chicks

Here are some cute fluffy chicks to celebrate Easter with. I like making a display by hanging these on branches arranged like a tree; it is easy and very cost-effective. You could also add them to an Easter bonnet or basket.

**1 Making the body** Cover your first polystyrene ball entirely with yellow wool, and attach it using the felting needle (see page 9). Hold the ball in one hand while you jab the wool into it with the other. You will hear a pleasing crunching noise as you push the wool into the ball.

## you will need

3 x polystyrene balls each 1½ in. (4 cm) diameter

¾ oz (20 g) merino wool tops in yellow

Felting needle with handle

¼ oz (5 g) merino wool tops in orange

⅛ oz (2 g) merino wool tops in black

Sewing needle

Sewing thread

Scissors

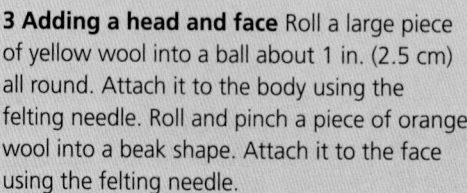

**2 Adding the wings** Roll up a piece of yellow wool to make a wing shape about 1 in. (2.5 cm) long. Attach it to the side of the ball body using your felting needle. Needle around the outer edge and gently over the top to make a curved shape. Add more wool if needed. Repeat on other side.

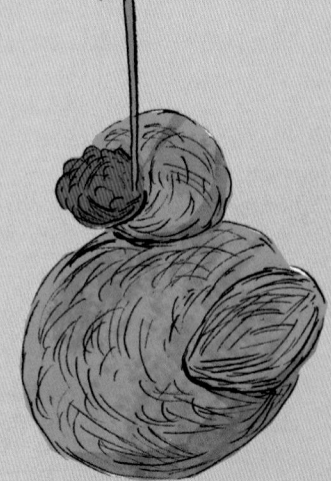

**3 Adding a head and face** Roll a large piece of yellow wool into a ball about 1 in. (2.5 cm) all round. Attach it to the body using the felting needle. Roll and pinch a piece of orange wool into a beak shape. Attach it to the face using the felting needle.

**4 Adding eyes** Roll a tiny piece of black wool into a ball and place on the chick's head. Poke it using the felting needle into a neat round eye shape, then repeat for the other eye.

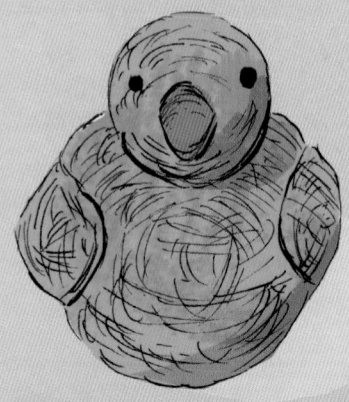

**5 Adding a hanging thread** If you would like to add a loop to hang your chick from, thread the sewing needle with thread, sew it through the back of the neck, and exit through the crown of the head. Tie a knot in the thread, and cover the knot by needling an extra piece of yellow wool over it. Repeat all the steps to make two more chicks.

# star bunting

Stars are used a lot in Nordic decorations, fabric, and knitting designs. This easy-to-make string of fabric stars can be used to decorate any room or could be made for a special occasion. You can choose different patterned fabric to suit the occasion: red and white fabric would be lovely for Christmas, or you could use offcuts that coordinate with bedroom furnishings for a funky accessory.

**1 Cutting out the stars** Use the cookie (biscuit) cutter as a guide and draw around it on your fabric with a soft pencil or chalk. Draw as many shapes as you like then cut out using small sharp scissors. I cut out 26 star shapes, to make 13 stars (lucky for some).

**2 Pairing the stars** Place the stars in pairs, with the front of the fabric facing outward. Pin together.

**3 Stitching the stars** Place the pair of stars on the sewing machine and sew straight across the center of each star, using a straight running stitch. Make a second line of stitching on some stars, to form a cross.

**4 Threading the stars** Thread the embroidery needle with the embroidery floss (thread) and knot at the end. Tie another knot about 4 in. (10 cm along) and thread through the first star. Tie another knot the same distance along, and thread through another star. Continue until all the stars are on and tie another slip knot at the end. Your star bunting is ready to hang.

## you will need

Star-shaped cookie (biscuit) cutter

Soft pencil or chalk

Scraps of fabric in assorted designs and colors

Small scissors

Pins

Sewing machine with white cotton thread

Embroidery needle

2 yd (2 m) white embroidery floss (thread)

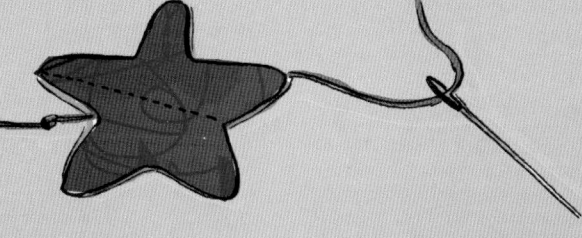

# pinecone folk

These charming pinecone people are a traditional make for Christmas time and will look lovely shimmering on the mantelpiece or hanging from your tree or Christmas display. Go for a wintery walk and take your time to select pinecones that are in good condition.

**1 Preparing a pinecone** Push the top of the pinecone down on a hard flat surface to flatten it and to check it can stand. If you need to, cut or twist off the tip to make it stable. This forms the base.

## you will need

Pinecones

Small paint brush

White, pink and blue acrylic paint

Handful of hazelnuts or almonds (in their shell)

Black fine tip permanent marker pen

Pva glue or a hot glue gun

Ready-made felt for the hat

Cotton thread to match felt

Sewing needle

4 in. (10 cm) ribbon for each scarf

Textured white yarn for scarf

Small bell

Glitter

**2 Painting** Paint the tips of the pinecone with white acrylic paint to give it a snowy effect and set aside to dry.

**3 Adding the face** Select a hazelnut or almond and paint a wide heart shape for the face using the white acrylic paint. When dry, use the marker pen to drawn on a face. Use the pink paint to add rosy cheeks, and blue paint for eyes. When the face is dry, glue the head on to the base of your pinecone (which is now at the top.) You might need to prop it against something to hold the head in place while the glue dries.

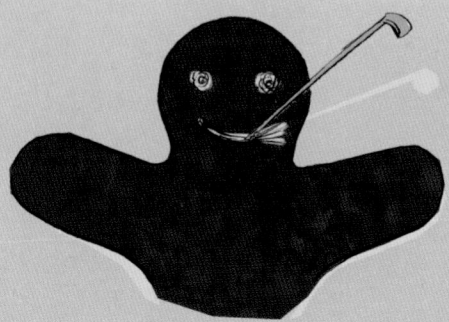

**3 Adding a smile** Pull off another piece of white wool and roll it with your fingers to make a long piece, the size of a smile. Using your felting needle, start at one end to attach the smile, pressing into the felt. Work the needle across to the other end of the mouth. Make sure the wool is completely felted by going over the edges with your needle.

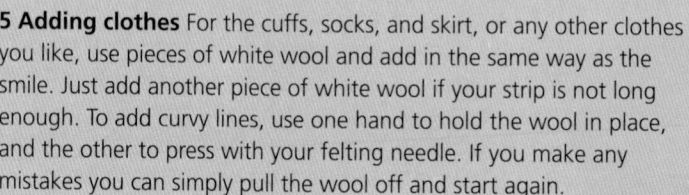

**4 Adding buttons** Pull off a small wisp of colored wool of your choice and roll into a ball. Add it to your person using the felting needle. Work your needle around the edges into a circular shape, to create a round button. Repeat this step for the other two buttons, using different colours.

**5 Adding clothes** For the cuffs, socks, and skirt, or any other clothes you like, use pieces of white wool and add in the same way as the smile. Just add another piece of white wool if your strip is not long enough. To add curvy lines, use one hand to hold the wool in place, and the other to press with your felting needle. If you make any mistakes you can simply pull the wool off and start again.

**6 Adding a hanging loop** Tie a piece of red and white string 8 in. (20 cm) to make a loop. Place the knot on the back of your gingerbread person and attach using a spare piece of brown wool and your felting needle. Repeat to make as many gingerbread people as you like!

**tip**
To make your own brown felt you will need a 35 x 20 in. (90 x 50 cm) piece of brown cotton muslin or gauze. Scatter over scraps of merino wool tops in ginger, dark brown, and light brown to add interest. During felting (see page 104) the fabric will shrink to roughly the size you need for this project.

To decorate the gingerbread house, add curvy lines, roof tiles, windows, and a door, following the method for adding buttons and clothes to the gingerbread people.

# christmas angels

These sweet little angels are so simple to make and look very effective hanging in the Christmas tree or from branches arranged in a vase. I love keeping my Christmas tree ornaments just white and red for a true Nordic look.

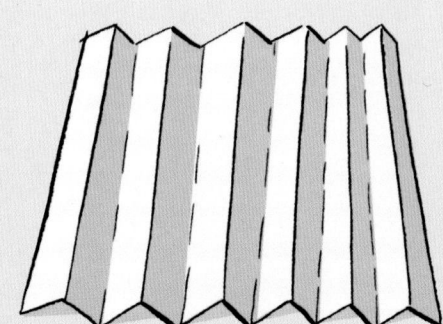

**1 Folding the fabric** Cut the Stitch 'n' Tear fabric into a rectangle approx 5 x 3 in. (12 x 7 cm). Fold it up into ½ in. (1 cm) folds.

## you will need

Selection of wooden beads

5 x 3 in. (12 x 7 cm) Stitch 'n' Tear fabric for each angel

Scissors

Sewing needle and white thread

Clear glue

**2 Making the arms** Cut a slit down the center of your piece of fabric, about 1 in. (2.5 cm) in length. Fold it up again, then fold down each side of the slit to create the angel's arms.

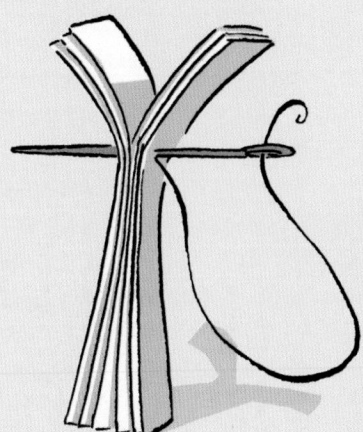

**3 Stitch the angel** Sew a few stitches on the fold underneath the arms, using white thread and a needle. This will strengthen the angel and help it to keep its shape.

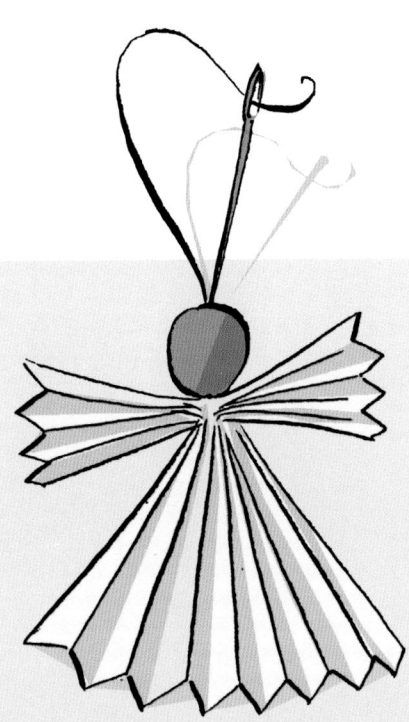

**4 Add a bead and hanger** Sew on a
wooden bead using about 8 in. (20 cm) of
white thread. This will leave you with enough
thread to tie a loop on top to make a hanger.
You can add clear glue underneath to hold
the bead in position. Repeat to make as many
angels as you like.

# christmas coronets

A Nordic Christmas would not be the same without "coronets", also known as cornettes or "kræmmerhus". You can make them any size you like, from large ones to hang at the end of the bed instead of stockings, or lots of small ones to use as an advent calendar, or as decorations. Fill with candy, or tiny presents!

**1 Cutting the fabric** Using the template on page 116, cut out one piece of fabric for the outside, and another for the lining of the coronet.

## you will need

Cotton fabric of your choice, e.g. spots or gingham

Plain cotton fabric for lining

Rikrak, bias tape, or ribbon

Sewing machine set with matching thread

Scissors

**2 Placing the handle** Cut a length of rikrak, bias tape, or ribbon for the handle about 5 in. (13 cm) long. Pin the handle to the top of the inside fabric shape on the right side, about 2 in (5cm) in from the edge on both sides (as marked on the template.)

**3 Sewing the coronet** Place the main fabric piece over the lining piece, with right sides together. Using a sewing machine threaded with matching thread, sew across the top using straight stitch, about ¼ in. (1 cm) from the top, attaching the handle as you sew.

## tip

You can make the coronets any size you like, by changing the enlargement ratio of the template. The marks on the template show you where to attach the handle.

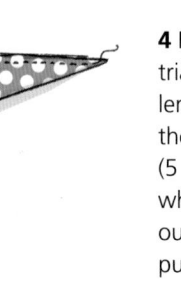

**4 Finishing the coronet** Open up the triangles, and then fold them in half lengthways with right sides facing. Sew over the edges, leaving a small gap of about 2 in. (5 cm) halfway down the lining, through which you then turn the coronet right-side out. You may need to use a pencil to help push out the fabric in the point of the coronet. Sew the gap closed using slip stitch.

**tip**

To make a handle from bias tape, cut the tape twice the length you want, fold in half lengthwise, and sew down the edge to make a thicker handle.

# index

# acknowledgments

First I would like to thank the whole team at CICO Books for all their hard work, a special thanks to Cindy Richards, Penny Craig and Becky Alexander for making it all come together perfectly. Thank you Michael Hill for the lovely illustrations. A big thank you goes to my beautiful mum and dad for all your help looking after Lilly and Eva while I worked on the many projects, I could not have done it without you. Thank you so much mum for your extensive knowledge in crafts, knitting and crochet, and for crocheting the baby blanket, and knitting the moss snoods and socks for this book. All your work is a work of art; you have a great eye for design a true inspiration. I'd like to thank my wonderful husband Harry for supporting me, and giving me two beautiful little girls. I would also like to send a big loving wave to my Danish, English, and Greek family, I love you all. Thanks to all my friends and family for all the encouragement, praise and keeping me sane throughout the course of this book. And, last but not least I want to thank again my fantastic Danish grandmother "mormor", Lilly Graversen. I will always think of you when I am making things I'm sure you would have loved this book and also *My Felted Friends*. All the projects I have made for these books are a celebration of you, you are the most amazing, loving, golden lady… I miss you.